FARM MACHINERY

LIFE ON THE FARM

Lynn M. Stone

Rourke Publishing LLC
Vero Beach, Florida 32964

www.rourkepublishing.com

PHOTO CREDITS:
Cover, p. 4, 7, 8, 10, 21 ©Lynn M. Stone. Title page, p. 12, 13, 15 17, 18 courtesy John Deere Photo Library

EDITORIAL SERVICES:
Pamela Schroeder

Library of Congress Cataloging-in-Publication Data

Stone, Lynn M.
    Farm machinery / Lynn M. Stone
      p. cm. — (Life on the farm)
    Includes bibliographical references
    Summary: Introduces various farm machines, including tractors and machines that help till, seed, and harvest crops.
    ISBN 1-58952-093-9
    1. Agricultural machinery—Juvenile literature. [1. Agricultural machinery. 2. Machinery.] I. Title.

S675.25 .S76 2001
631.3—dc21   20010321671

Printed in the USA

TABLE OF CONTENTS

FARM MACHINERY

Farm **machines** do many of the jobs farmers once did on their own. But machines do farm jobs much faster.

Farm machines are built in many sizes and shapes. All of them have some moving parts. Some have motors.

Farm machines do many special jobs. Some machines work alone. Others work with tractors.

The tractor became the farmer's "iron horse" in the 20th century. This is a tractor from the 1950s.

Farm work used to be done with work animals and hand tools. Until the mid-1800s there were no farm machines with engines. There were few machines of any kind. Farmers used horses, mules, and **oxen** to help with field work.

Farmers used to be able to grow only enough for their families. With machines, they could grow enough food to sell.

Farmers and their teams of horses used to do the farm work now done by machines.

TRACTORS

A tractor does many jobs on the farm. Its big, **rugged** tires help it move over rough, muddy, or snowy ground.

A tractor can be used with other farm machines and tools. It can pull machines such as seed drills, plows, planters, and hay **balers**. Farmers can add steel arms to lift heavy things.

The tractor driver can work all these machines from inside the tractor.

Modern tractors are big, rugged machines that can easily be fitted with other farm machines.

9

TILLAGE MACHINES

Making soil ready for seeds is called **tilling**. This is the first step in planting. Tillage machines do the tilling.

One important tillage machine is the disc. A disc has many plate-shaped blades. The blades turn like wheels when the disc is being pulled. The blades turn up and loosen the soil.

Tillage machines with steel blades loosen and break up soil.

A mowing machine works like a giant lawn mower to cut field grasses like hay.

This hay baler wraps cut hay into big, round bales.

Other types of tillage machines cut through old crop plants and smash lumps of soil. The chisel plow is one of these heavyweight tillers. Light discs smooth out the soil.

The round blades of this disc cut into soil to help prepare it for planting.

SEEDING MACHINES

Seeding machines plant seeds in soil. The corn planter is one of the most widely used seeding machines. The corn planter has round, side-by-side blades. They cut a V-shaped **furrow** in the ground. Furrows are planting rows in a field.

The corn planter drops seeds into the furrow one at a time. As it moves along, the planter also covers the seeds with soil. The furrow can be as deep as the farmer wants the planter to make it.

Seeding machines dig furrows and drop seeds into them. They also cover the furrows with soil.

With small changes, corn planters can also be used to plant soybean, pumpkin, and cotton seeds.

The drill is another seeding machine. The drill is used to plant small grains such as rice, oats, wheat, and barley. It's also used for soybeans.

Sprayers can water crops or spray weed-killing chemicals onto them.

HARVEST MACHINES

Harvest machines gather fruits, vegetables, and other farm plants when they are ripe. Tractors pull some harvest machines. Others work under their own power.

The **combine** is a harvester with its own power. Combines can be used to harvest crops such as corn, soybeans, and dry beans.

A corn combine harvests corn ears, shucks them, and cleans kernels off the cob.

The combine rumbles through standing corn like a train. It rips ears of corn from their stalks. It rubs the corn kernels off the stalk and shoots them into a bin. It does all this without stopping!

Balers gather cut hay and pack it into **bales**. Bales may be round or in blocks. Some weigh about 2,000 pounds (909 kilograms).

GLOSSARY

bales (BAYLZ) — bundles of hay or straw

baler (BAYL er) — a machine that gathers up and packs hay into bales

combine (KAHM byn) — a machine that harvests grain

furrow (FUR oh) — a V-shaped garden or field row in which seeds are planted

harvest (HAR vist) — having to do with the gathering of ripe oats; the crop itself

machines (meh SHEENZ) — a group of moving parts that work together to do a job

oxen (AHK sen) — male cattle tamed and used to pull heavy loads

rugged (RUG id) — rough and tough

tilling (TIL ing) — making fields ready for planting

INDEX

Further Reading

Armentrout, David & Patricia. *Farm Machinery*. Rourke Publishing, 1995.
Bushey, Jerry. *Farming the Land: Modern Farmers and Their Machines*. Lerner, 1993
Pang, Alex (illustrator). *Trucks, Tractors and Cranes*. Millbrook, 2000

Websites To Visit

www.deere.com/deerecom_kids
www.historylink101.com/news/teacher_resources

About The Author

Lynn Stone is the author of more than 400 children's books. He is a talented natural history photographer as well. Lynn, a former teacher, travels worldwide to photograph wildlife in its natural habitat.